Wrestling the ABC's

ACTIVITY BOOK VOLUME ONE

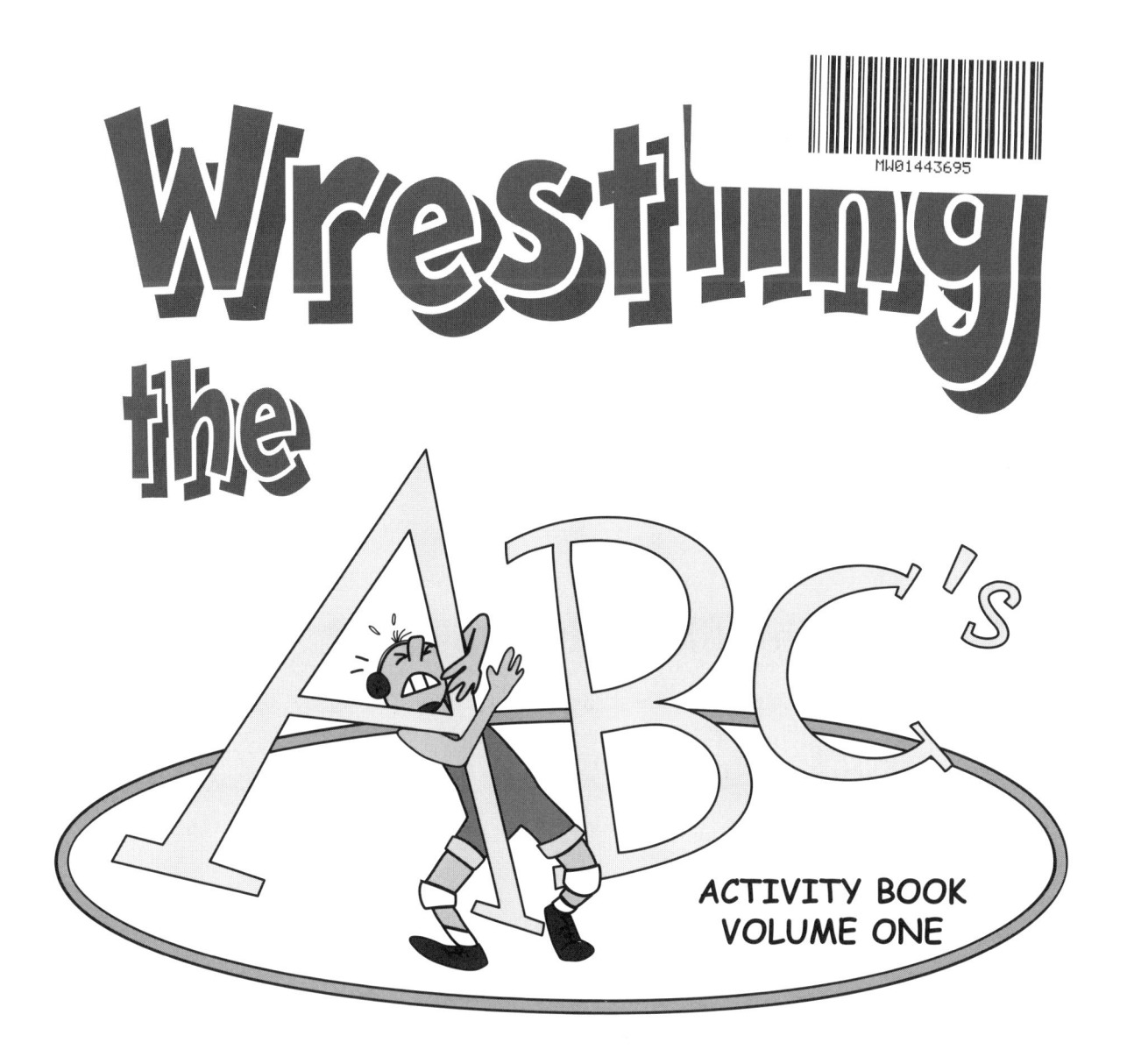

Tom and Veronica Davids
Illustrations by Robert Lence

GOLD MEDAL PUBLISHING
www.wrestlingtheabcs.com

Published by Davids Gold Medal Sports
23809 John R. Rd., Hazel Park, MI 48030
© 2008 by Tom and Veronica Davids
Illustrations © 2008 by Robert Lence

Printed in Canada

ISBN - 13: 978-0-9817554-0-3
ISBN - 10: 0-9817554-0-2

For information about this activity book or its parent book, <u>Wrestling the ABC's</u>, a picture book for wrestling fans of all ages, please contact Davids Gold Medal Sports at 1-888-RESTLER or email: wrestlingtheabcs@mac.com, or visit the website at http://www.wrestlingtheabcs.com

Introduction

Puzzles are fun. Puzzles about wrestling are even more fun! And the "surprise inside" is that these puzzles are great learning tools too! This activity book features a wide variety of puzzles and games that will appeal to the wrestling fan in everyone. Enjoy these visual, numerical and language puzzles while having fun with wrestling!

Fondly,

Tom and Veronica Davids

CONGRATULATIONS!!!
COUPON OF COMPLETION
(ACTIVITY BOOK-VOLUME ONE)

DEAR WRESTLING FRIEND,

Thank you for purchasing our activity book. Upon completion, please fill out this form, and bring in to Davids' Gold Medal Sports for $1.00 off the picture book, Wrestling The ABC's! Or, order the book online (no need to fill out the form). Online orders will also receive $1.00 off the book (enter code word: wrestler)

Your Name_____
Your Age_____
Favorite Puzzle (page #)_____
Did you like this book?_____
Will you consider buying volume two?_____
www.wrestlingtheabcs.com

Lone Letter

Each line in the box has one letter that is different from the others. Circle that letter. Then write it in the correct space below. Do the same thing for each line and you will find a wrestling word.

1.	L	L	T	L	L	L	L	L
2.	A	P	P	P	P	P	P	P
3.	R	R	R	R	R	K	R	R
4.	W	W	W	W	E	W	W	W
5.	M	D	M	M	M	M	M	M
6.	Y	Y	Y	Y	Y	Y	O	Y
7.	C	C	C	W	C	C	C	C
8.	L	L	L	L	L	L	L	N

__ __ __ __ __ __ __ __
1   2   3   4   5   6   7   8

Changing Letters

Change each letter to the one that comes right before it in the alphabet. Write the new letters in the spaces above the originals to find some words of wisdom from a famous wrestler and coach.

Here's a copy of the alphabet to help you:

ABCDEFGHIJKLMNOPQRSTUVWXYZ

___ ___ ___ ___ _____,
PODF ZPV I BWF XSFTUMFE

_____ ____ ____ __ ____
FWFSZUIJOH FMTF JO MJGF

__ ____.
JT FBTZ.

Dan Gable,

Olympic Gold Medalist,
renowned wrestling coach.

Unscramble

Unscramble these wrestling words. Then place the boxed letters in the spaces below to finish the sentence.

1. DMLGDOELA   _ _ _ _ _ M☐ _ _ _
2. TWNDEKAO   _☐K _ _ _ _ _
3. LSRWERET   _ _ _ _ ☐L _ _ _
4. HSPPSUU   _ _ _ ☐H _ _ _
5. ZERIWZ   W _ _ _ ☐ _
6. TMA   _☐ _
7. ILTNEGS   _ _ _ _ ☐ _ T
8. PNSOTI   _ _ _ N☐ _
9. HCCOA   _ _ _ C☐
10. LTEFRESYE   _ _ _ E _ _☐ _
11. ERFREEE   _ _☐E _ _ _
12. MNGERCROOA   _ _ _ C _☐ _☐ _ _
13. ADAREEHG   _ _ A☐ _ _ _
14. PKACJJMUNGIS   _ _ _ _ I _ _ _ C _☐

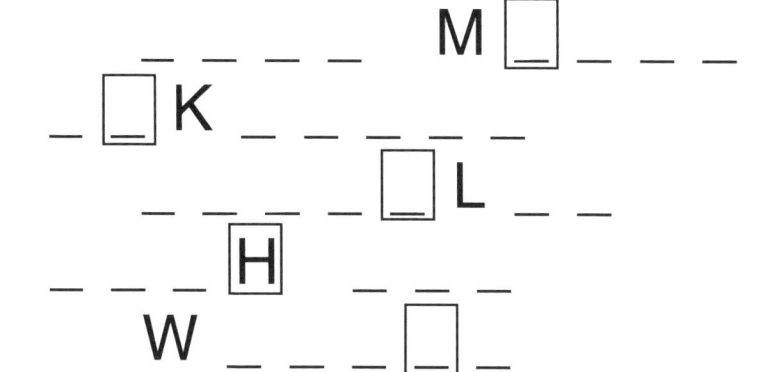

To become a champion in any sport you should always ...

_ _ _ H _ _ _ _ _ _ _ _ _ _ _

7

Wrestling Word Search

Find these wrestling moves in the puzzle below.

ARM DRAG ESCAPE   NEARFALL   REVERSAL
FIREMANS PIN   HEADLOCK   HALF NELSON
ANKLE PICK LEG LACE TAKEDOWN   SNAP DOWN

A	P	I	N	P	N	R	H	R	A	G	A	D
E	S	C	A	N	E	E	E	K	R	E	C	Y
D	E	S	C	A	A	V	A	E	M	A	I	M
L	S	K	H	G	R	E	D	Y	D	R	N	M
E	C	P	Y	O	F	R	L	W	R	L	O	O
G	A	R	Z	L	A	S	O	E	A	I	R	T
L	P	S	Z	P	L	A	C	H	G	P	E	W
A	E	A	I	D	L	L	K	C	A	S	V	A
C	H	A	L	F	N	E	L	S	O	N	X	A
E	N	N	C	L	T	A	K	E	D	O	W	N
F	I	R	E	M	A	N	S	E	S	C	A	P
U	L	U	L	L	S	N	A	P	D	O	W	N
E	A	F	E	N	O	T	G	N	I	M	E	R
X	Z	B	C	A	N	K	L	E	P	I	C	K

8

The Thrill Of Victory

What Am I?

For each clue, write the word that is in all **capital** letters in the blanks on the next page. Put the letters that are circled in the blank spaces at the bottom to reveal the answer to the puzzle.

1. I come in many **COLORS**.
2. I am part of a wrestler's **UNIFORM**.
3. I fit **SNUG**.
4. I am worn by **GIRLS** and boys.
5. Sometimes I am **REVERSIBLE**.
6. I am made of **STRETCHY** fabric.
7. I am worn in all **STYLES** of wrestling.

3. SNUG

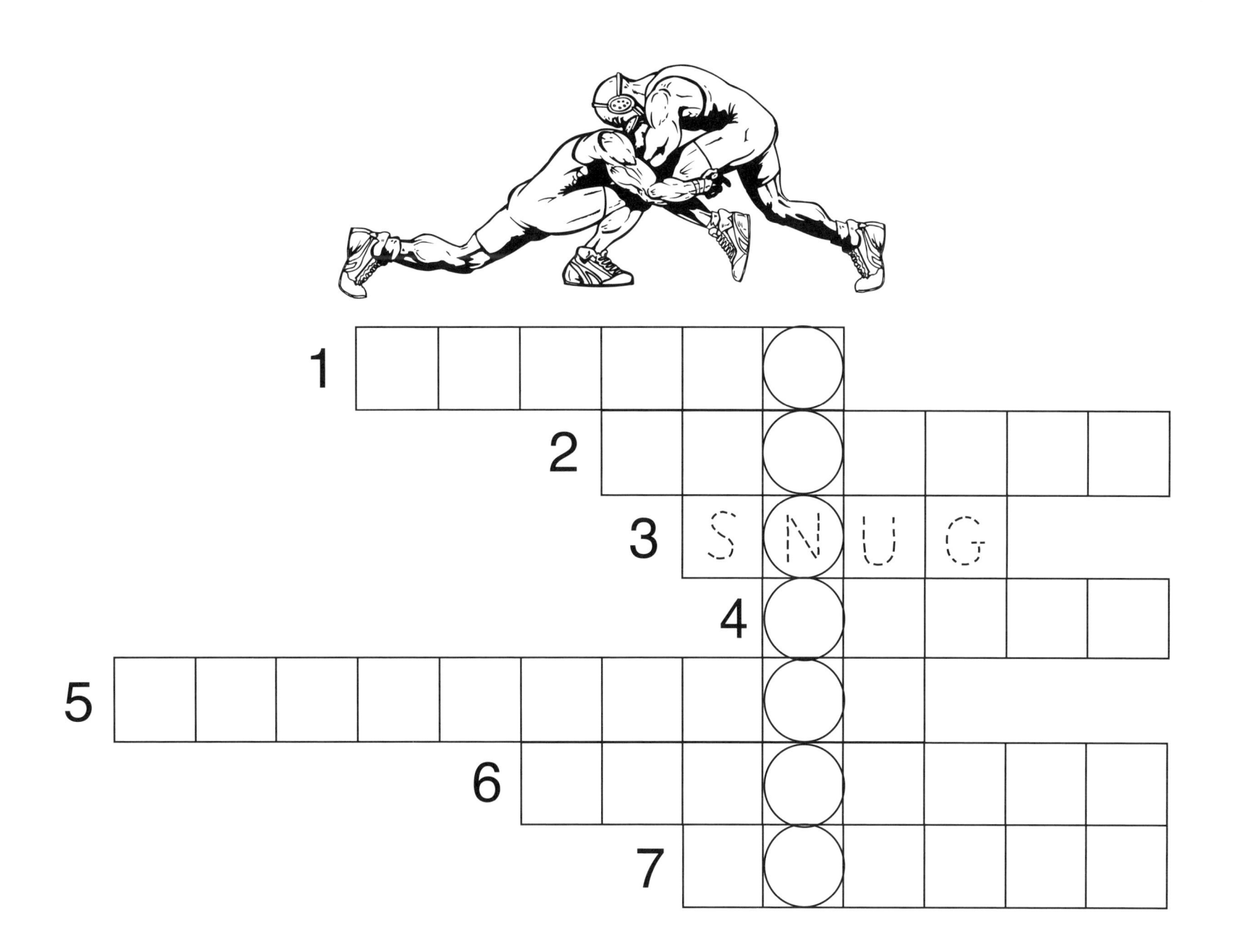

I am a

___ ___ N ___ ___ ___ ___ ___

11

Find these healthy foods hidden in the puzzle below.
A little tougher, there are some backwards and diagonal.

BANANAS	WATER	CHEESE	ORANGES
CORN	APPLES	GRAPES	BAGELS
PEAS	RAISINS	MILK	CARROTS

B	S	A	S	R	P	N	W	A	T	E	E	R	M
A	G	R	A	P	E	G	E	P	E	A	S	A	S
N	O	B	I	G	K	B	A	G	I	L	S	L	E
A	A	N	A	N	A	B	S	E	A	G	E	S	R
N	O	B	N	N	S	L	E	N	G	G	S	R	A
N	B	A	G	S	A	R	G	P	A	T	A	A	A
A	S	E	L	P	A	N	N	B	O	C	R	T	S
S	G	R	A	P	E	S	A	R	A	S	N	I	R
A	P	P	L	E	S	A	R	S	I	N	S	R	R
E	S	E	E	H	C	A	O	A	N	I	E	C	I
S	R	O	P	I	C	L	R	S	R	S	G	O	S
E	G	P	K	L	I	M	G	E	S	I	N	R	O
A	E	L	P	P	A	S	T	E	C	A	A	N	R
G	A	A	P	G	K	A	H	N	R	R	R	O	O
E	A	A	A	A	W	C	R	N	R	P	O	A	W

12

Connect The Dots

Use your pencil to connect the dots in numerical order. Start at number one and color it when you're done!

13

Trace The Wrestling Words

head and arm throw

sprawl out quickly

double leg takedown

read a lot of books

Olympic Champion

have determination

give it your very best

show sportsmanship

Uppercase Puzzle

1.	S	v	b	W	o	I	T	k	k	C	p	j	H
2.	k	S	s	I	c	D	s	E	R	O	c	L	L
3.	S	c	T	A	e	N	g	b	D	U	m	e	P
4.	G	k	R	m	A	N	s	a	B	t	o	Y	e
5.	w	P	E	T	y	h	E	R	u	w	S	O	N
6.	T	E	c	t	C	H	o	F	c	A	L	q	L
7.	A	R	h	x	M	a	S	P	i	l	x	N	u
8.	A	k	y	R	M	c	e	e	B	A	n	n	R
9.	C	a	R	O	k	S	S	p	F	A	g	C	E
10.	G	d	t	U	T	W	R	E	b	N	C	f	H

Circle all of the capital, or **UPPERCASE** letters in each row. Write them on the lines below to spell some wrestling techniques.

1. _ _ _ _ _ _
2. _ _ _ _   _ _ _ _ _
3. _ _ _ _ _   _ _
4. _ _ _ _ _ _
5. _ _ _ _ _ _ _ _

6. _ _ _ _   _ _ _ _
7. _ _ _   _ _ _ _
8. _ _ _   _ _ _
9. _ _ _ _ _   _ _ _ _
10. _ _ _   _ _ _ _ _

15

Wrestling Around the World

Every four years Olympic wrestlers go for the gold medal. Match the numbers on the map to the Olympic Games host city.

1960 - ROME, ITALY ____
1964 - TOKYO, JAPAN ____
1968 - MEXICO CITY, MEXICO ____
1972 - MUNICH, GERMANY ____
1976 - MONTREAL, CANADA ____
1980 - MOSCOW, RUSSIA ____
1984 - LOS ANGELES, USA ____
1988 - SEOUL, SOUTH KOREA ____
1992 - BARCELONA, SPAIN ____
1996 - ATLANTA, USA ____
2000 - SYDNEY, AUSTRALIA ____
2004 - ATHENS, GREECE ____
2008 - BEIJING, CHINA ____
2012 - LONDON, ENGLAND ____

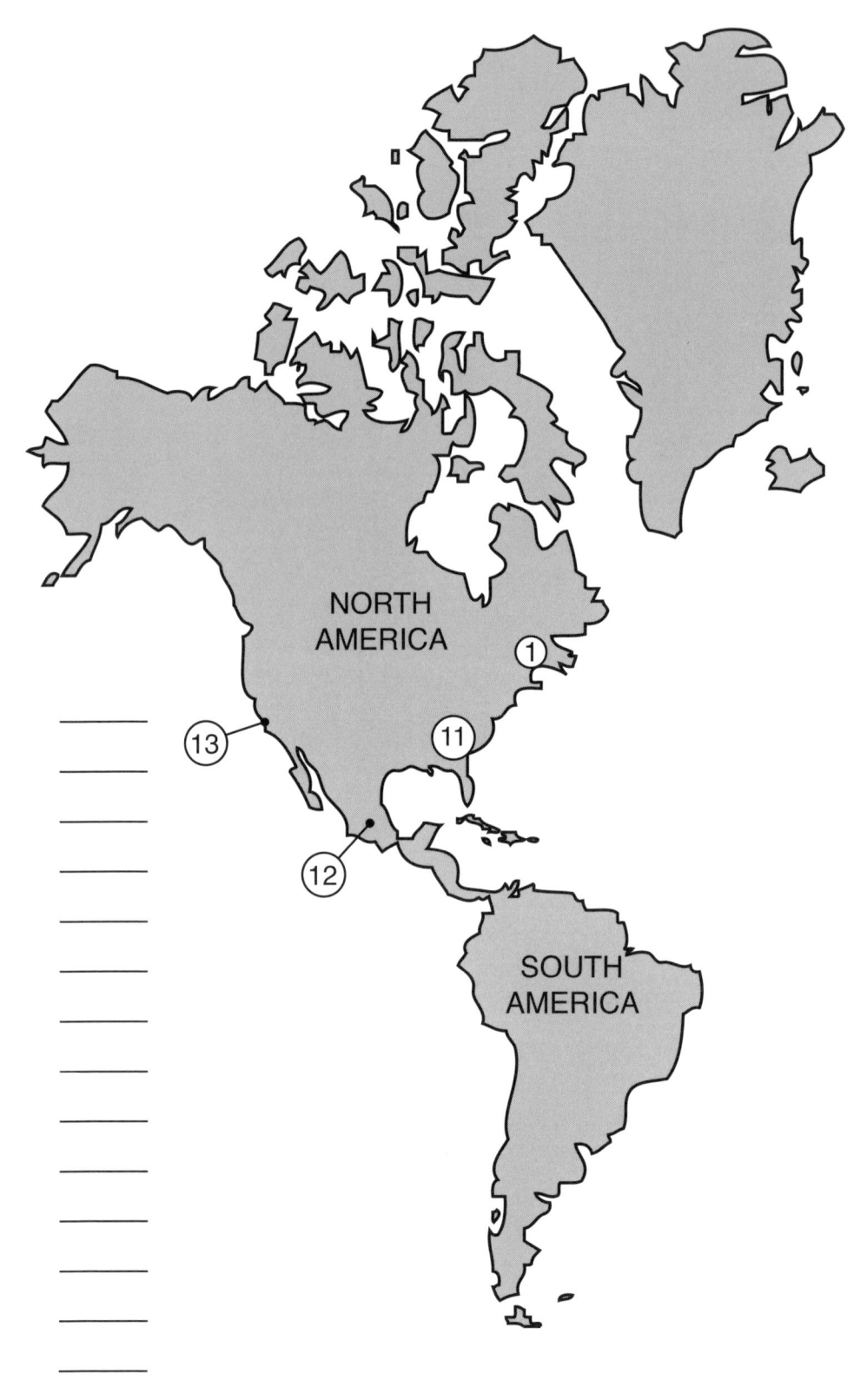

1. On how many continents have the Olympic Games been held since 1960? _____

2. Which continent has hosted the Olympic Games the most times since 1960? _____

3. Which country has hosted the Olympic Games the most times since 1960 ? _____

17

Wrestling Word Search

Find the wrestling equipment words hidden in the puzzle below.

KNEEPADS SCOREBOOK JUMP ROPE
HEADGEAR MAT SCOREBOARD
DUFFLE BAG SHOES SINGLET
WHISTLE SOCKS MOUTHGUARD

S	O	C	S	M	A	T	K	K	M	I
K	R	S	O	C	K	S	E	L	O	C
S	C	O	R	E	B	O	O	K	U	M
O	K	S	M	P	O	S	A	D	T	O
W	N	I	A	Y	H	C	N	U	H	O
H	E	N	T	L	E	O	K	F	G	J
I	E	G	S	O	A	R	L	F	U	U
S	P	L	I	T	D	E	E	L	A	M
T	A	E	N	K	G	B	P	E	R	P
L	D	T	G	S	E	O	I	B	D	R
E	S	T	P	W	A	A	C	A	D	O
S	H	O	E	S	R	R	K	G	O	P
K	F	G	T	H	C	D	D	L	G	E

18

Coloring Fun

Drilling double legs

Trace The Wrestling Words

wrestling is fun

drill all your moves

respect the referees

set goals   aim high

eat healthy food

have a good plan

get plenty of sleep

wrestlers are winners

Back Space

Add one letter to the end of each letter group to form the word that solves the clue. Then read DOWN to find the word that describes a group of exercises.

A referee may flip one of these	DIS____
This fish is used to make sandwiches	TUN____
Hold his or her back to the mat to earn this	NEARFAL____
You can do this on a hill in the snow	SK____
A serious and aggressive competitor is	TENACIOU____
You wrestle on top of this	MA____
When you work with numbers you're doing	MAT____
When you get away from your opponent	ESCAP____
It always ends a wrestling match	PI____
This is called the "Aloha State"	HAWAI____
Stay calm-don't do this	PANI____
This is a fun move to do	HIP TOS____

Make A Word

Follow the directions to find seven letters in the grid. After you find a letter, write it in the blank space on each line. Then read down to find what every wrestler is.

FIND THE LETTER:
1. That is below the **+** _____
2. That is between the **#** and the **=** _____
3. That is above the **?** _____
4. That is to the left of the **!** _____
5. That is to the right of the **=** _____
6. That is to the right of the ***** _____
7. That is to the left of the **@** _____

+	X	E	@	H
A	M	#	P	?
R	O	T	Q	V
B	Y	=	E	S
L	!	K	*	T

22

Wrestling Legend

On each line look at the word in the left column. Then look at the word in the right column. The word in the left column contains one more letter than the word in the right column. Write this additional letter in the blank space in the center. When you are done, read down the center to find the name of a famous wrestler and coach.

MEDALS	___	MEALS
SALAMI	___	ISLAM
INFANT	___	FAINT

GROUND	___	ROUND
PARADE	___	DRAPE
TABLE	___	LATE
CRADLE	___	RACED
STREAM	___	SMART

23

True OR False

Read each sentence. If the sentence is TRUE, circle the letter in the true column. If the sentence is FALSE, circle the letter in the false column. When you have finished, write the circled letters in the blank spaces below to solve the puzzle.

		TRUE	FALSE
1.	Girls aren't allowed to wrestle.	J	O
2.	Junk food will make you strong.	V	L
3.	A pin will end a wrestling match.	Y	S
4.	Wrestling mats are made of steel.	T	M
5.	A kilogram is a kind of cracker.	A	P
6.	Sometimes wrestlers win medals.	I	T
7.	Skinny kids shouldn't try wrestling.	E	C
8.	Wrestling shoes are different than tennis shoes.	S	P

Many wrestlers dream of wrestling in the:

__ __ __ __ __ __ __ __

Spy a Letter

Look at the words on line one. The letter "C" is only used once. We have written the letter "C" in the blank space above the number one. Find the letters that are only used once on each line and write them in on the lines below to solve the riddle.

What wrestling move should you put your opponent in if they are acting like a baby?

1. BAT   CAT   TAB
2. TAM   MAT   RAT
3. OAT   TOP   POT
4. LATE TALE DATE
5. LAD   DAM   MAD
6. RAM   ARM   EAR

ANSWER:

$\dfrac{C}{1}\ \dfrac{}{2}\ \dfrac{}{3}\ \dfrac{}{4}\ \dfrac{}{5}\ \dfrac{}{6}$

25

Funny Names

Some wrestling moves have funny names. Write the name of the object pictured in the blank spaces to reveal the names of some wrestling moves and terms.

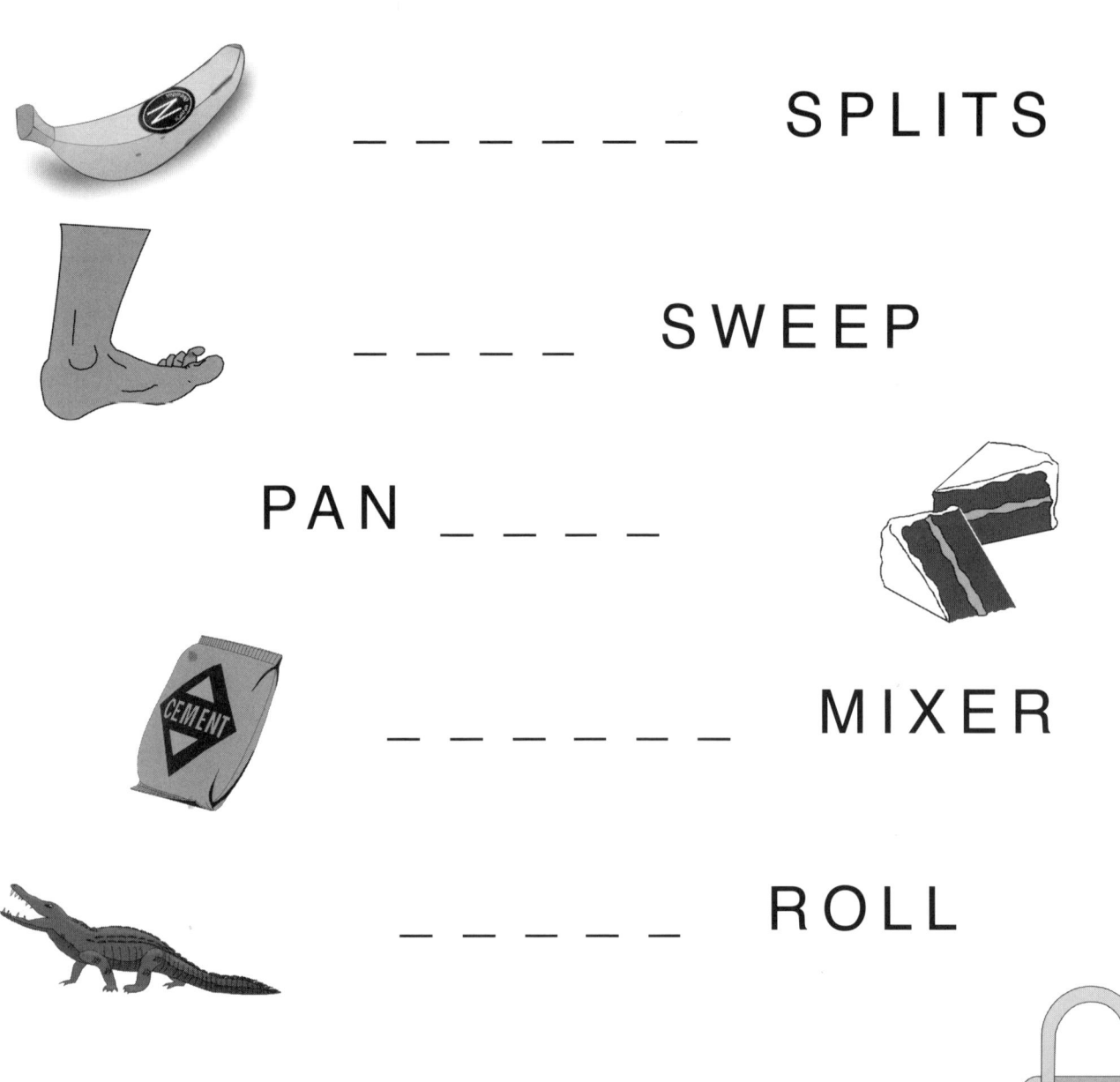

_ _ _ _ _ _ SPLITS

_ _ _ _ SWEEP

PAN _ _ _ _

_ _ _ _ _ _ MIXER

_ _ _ _ _ ROLL

HEAD _ _ _ _

26

🦆 _ _ _ _ UNDER

✝️😐 _ _ _ _ _   _ _ _ _ CRADLE

🐔 _ _ _ _ _ _ _ _ WING

ANKLE _ _ _ _ ⛏️

LEG _ _ _ _ _ _ _ _ _ ✂️

🧷 _ _ _ TO WIN!

27

Changing Letters

Change each letter to the one that comes right before it in the alphabet. Write the new letters in the spaces above the originals to find some words of inspiration from a famous wrestler and coach. Here's a copy of the alphabet to help you:

ABCDEFGHIJKLMNOPQRSTUVWXYZ

$\overline{\text{W}}\,\overline{\text{I}}\,\overline{\text{T}}\,\overline{\text{H}}$ $\overline{\text{P}}\,\overline{\text{A}}\,\overline{\text{S}}\,\overline{\text{S}}\,\overline{\text{I}}\,\overline{\text{O}}\,\overline{\text{N}}$ $\overline{\text{A}}\,\overline{\text{N}}\,\overline{\text{D}}$ $\overline{\text{H}}\,\overline{\text{A}}\,\overline{\text{R}}\,\overline{\text{D}}$
X J U I   Q B T T J P O   B O E   I B S E

$\overline{\text{W}}\,\overline{\text{O}}\,\overline{\text{R}}\,\overline{\text{K}}$, $\overline{\text{Y}}\,\overline{\text{O}}\,\overline{\text{U}}$ $\overline{\text{N}}\,\overline{\text{E}}\,\overline{\text{V}}\,\overline{\text{E}}\,\overline{\text{R}}$ $\overline{\text{K}}\,\overline{\text{N}}\,\overline{\text{O}}\,\overline{\text{W}}$,
X P S L,   Z P V   O F W F S   L O P X,

$\overline{\text{Y}}\,\overline{\text{O}}\,\overline{\text{U}}\,\overline{\text{R}}$ $\overline{\text{D}}\,\overline{\text{R}}\,\overline{\text{E}}\,\overline{\text{A}}\,\overline{\text{M}}\,\overline{\text{S}}$ $\overline{\text{M}}\,\overline{\text{A}}\,\overline{\text{Y}}$ $\overline{\text{C}}\,\overline{\text{O}}\,\overline{\text{M}}\,\overline{\text{E}}$ $\overline{\text{T}}\,\overline{\text{R}}\,\overline{\text{U}}\,\overline{\text{E}}$!
Z P V S   E S F B N T   N B Z   D P N F   U S V F!

Zeke Jones,

Childhood dreamer,
World Champion
Olympic Silver Medalist

Wrestling Match

The small pictures at the bottom of the page are all part of the larger one at the top of the page. Can you tell where each piece came from? Find the letter and number of the box where the small picture is located and write it in the blank space under each picture. We have done one for you. Have fun!

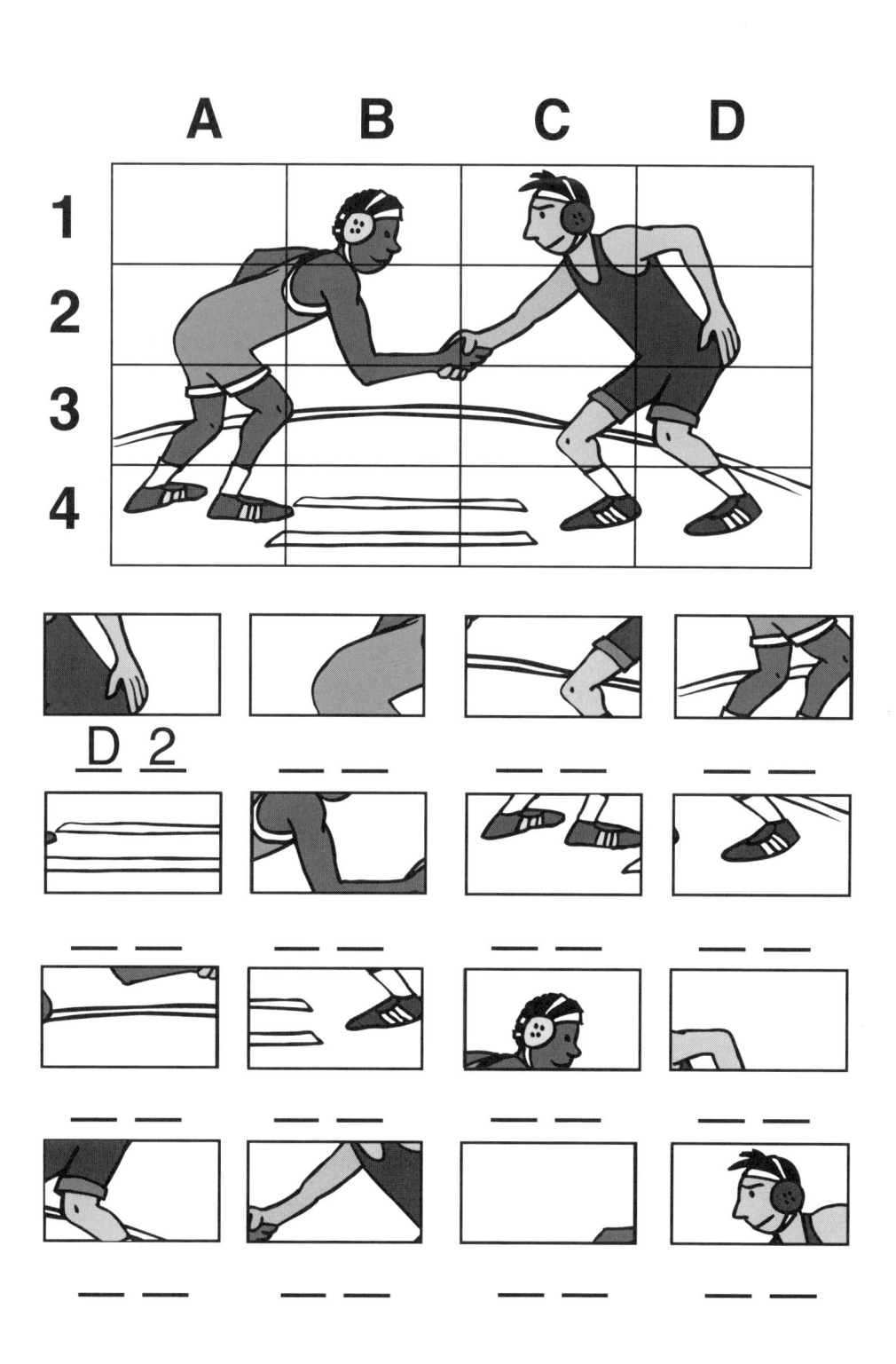

D 2

Puzzle Answers

Page 5
LONE LETTER

TAKEDOWN

Page 6
CHANGING LETTERS

ONCE YOU HAVE WRESTLED, EVERYTHING ELSE IN LIFE IS EASY

Page 7
UNSCRAMBLE

1. GOLD MEDAL
2. TAKEDOWN
3. WRESTLER
4. PUSH UPS
5. WIZZER
6. MAT
7. SINGLET
8. POINTS
9. COACH
10. FREESTYLE
11. REFEREE
12. GRECO ROMAN
13. HEADGEAR
14. JUMPING JACKS

EAT HEALTHY FOODS

Page 8
WORDSEARCH

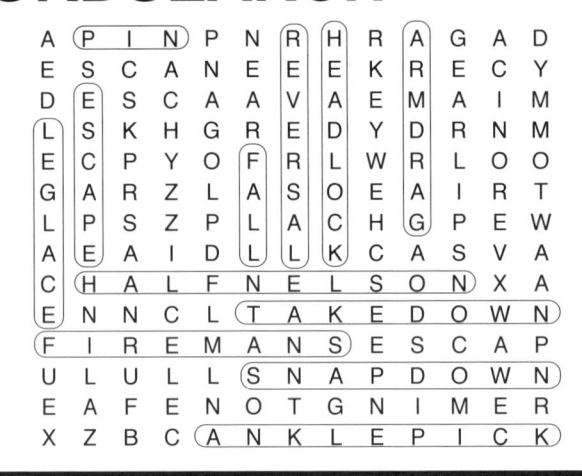

Pages 10 and 11
WHAT AM I?

I AM A SINGLET

Page 12
WORDSEARCH

30

Page 15
UPPERCASE PUZZLE

1. SWITCH
2. SIDE ROLL
3. STAND UP
4. GRANBY
5. PETERSON
6. TECH FALL
7. ARM SPIN
8. ARM BAR
9. CROSS FACE
10. GUT WRENCH

Pages 16 and 17
WRESTLING AROUND THE WORLD

1960 - ROME, ITALY	7
1964 - TOKYO, JAPAN	8
1968 - MEXICO CITY, MEXICO	12
1972 - MUNICH, GERMANY	2
1976 - MONTREAL, CANADA	1
1980 - MOSCOW, RUSSIA	5
1984 - LOS ANGELES, USA	13
1988 - SEOUL, SOUTH KOREA	6
1992 - BARCELONA, SPAIN	9
1996 - ATLANTA, USA	11
2000 - SYDNEY, AUSTRALIA	14
2004 - ATHENS, GREECE	3
2008 - BEIJING, CHINA	4
2012 - LONDON, ENGLAND	10

Pages 16 and 17 continued:
WRESTLING AROUND THE WORLD

1. Four continents-Asia, Australia, Europe and North America
2. Europe
3. United States of America (USA)-two times

Page 18
WORDSEARCH

Page 21
BACKSPACE
CALISTHENICS

Page 22
MAKE A WORD
ATHLETE

31

Page 23
WRESTLING LEGEND

DAN GABLE

Page 24
TRUE OR FALSE

OLYMPICS

Page 25
SPY A LETTER

CRADLE

Page 26
FUNNY NAMES

BANANA SPLITS, **FOOT** SWEEP, PAN**CAKE**, **CEMENT** MIXER, **GATOR** ROLL, HEAD **LOCK**

Page 27
FUNNY NAMES

DUCK UNDER, **CROSS FACE** CRADLE, **CHICKEN** WING, **ANKLE** PICK, LEG **SCISSORS**, **PIN** TO WIN

Page 28
CHANGING LETTERS

WITH PASSION AND HARD WORK, YOU NEVER KNOW, YOUR DREAMS MAY COME TRUE!

Page 29
WRESTLING MATCH

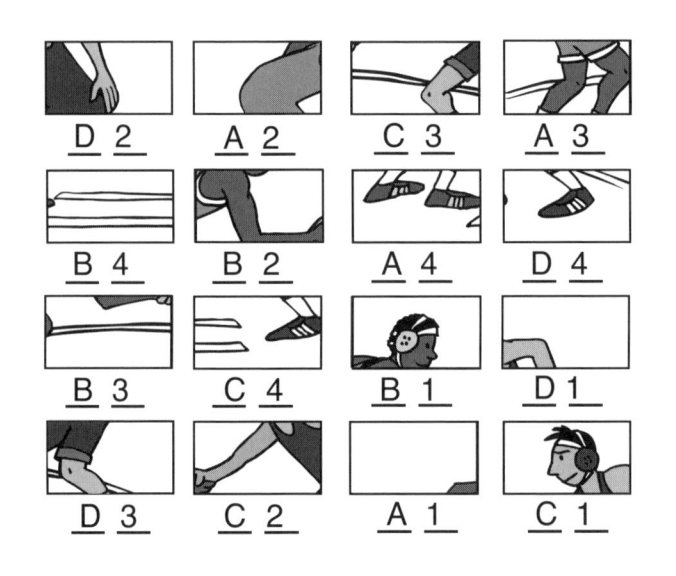

D 2	A 2	C 3	A 3
B 4	B 2	A 4	D 4
B 3	C 4	B 1	D 1
D 3	C 2	A 1	C 1